Anyone who's worked with John Spencer knows how refreshing his bloody-minded contrariness and mischievous wordplay can be.

This book is a collection of soundbites from John's published writings on graphic design that strip away the nonsense to reveal common sense. His thoughts are grenades of sanity lobbed into an industry that has mythologised creativity.

There's no bullsh*t like design bullsh*t will provoke and be enjoyed by design students, agencies, clients and everyone who would like to communicate better.

Tom Lynham
International Wordstorming

liberating

Embrace
constraints –
you'll be
surprised
how

it is

Design without boundaries is pointless

Look
for
the

It
surprises
most
of
the
people
most
of
the
time.

You've heard the adage 'a picture is worth a thousand words'. Well, it's not always true. Sometimes a few well-written words are worth more than any picture.

obvious.

Design
is a
point
of
view

A lot of people believe young designers have
all the best ideas, but it's not so. There are two
kinds of creativity: conceptual and experimental.
Conceptual designers do their best work early
in their careers, while experimental designers
develop over time. Good ideas have nothing
to do with age.

Ad e sig n er's jo bist om a kes ens e oft hin gs

People value what they under stand

Everybody knows the hackneyed catchphrase 'think outside the box'. It means to think differently or unconventionally and look beyond the obvious. Well here's a novel idea: think inside the box. You'll be amazed by the things you've missed.

Brainstorming is the most popular creativity technique of all time. There's just one problem: it doesn't work. Decades of scientific research have shown that people have far better ideas when they work on their own and share their thoughts later. Brainstorms stifle originality.

Design isn't hard –
just play around with
ideas as they occur
to you.

The playing is easy—
it's the occurring
that's hard.

Everything an organisation says and does,
and the way it looks, needs to be so individual
that it just can't be mistaken for any other. Its
idiosyncrasies need to be uncovered, given
form and voice, and ruthlessly protected.

Idiosyncratic + ruth

ess = unforgettable

Trust your instinct. It's usually right.

Science has shattered the myth that creativity is a gift only some of us have. Research shows that everyone is born with the ability to think creatively. You don't have to be a 'creative type' to be creative.

Process is the heartbeat of design

People often think design is all about being inventive, ingenious and inspired. This is perpetuated by the design industry, and it's nonsense. Design legend Alan Fletcher captured the down-to-earthness of what we do when he talked about graphic designers as the blue-collar workers of the art world. But American painter and photographer Chuck Close nailed it when he said: "Inspiration is for amateurs. The rest of us just show up and get to work."

Listen

While I was a graphics student I worked at Pentagram for a couple of weeks. I have a vivid memory of Alan Fletcher doing my portfolio review – it was Plymouth Boy meets the Father of British Graphic Design. "You're just pissing about," he said. It was a bruising encounter with reality.

unexpected Take advantage of the

Know when to sto   p

Language and design are indivisible

Everyone's heard the cliché 'less is more'. It's about how simplicity leads to good design. Architect Mies van der Rohe adopted it as his minimalist motto. Futurist Buckminster Fuller reinvented it as 'doing more with less'. And industrial designer Dieter Rams paraphrased it as 'less but better'. Less is more is an absurd idea. Less is just less. Graphic designer Milton Glaser's 'just enough is more' makes a lot more sense.

Brand dynamics...brand awareness...brand loyalty...brand commitment...brand archetype... brand positioning...brand engagement...brand fingerprint...brand purpose...brand personality... brand champion...brand architecture...brand essence...brand footprint...brand ambassador... brand harmonisation...brand discovery...brand proposition...brand elasticity...brand promise... Let's get over our obsession with brand and get on with making good, honest design.

Bullsh*t bamboozles people and makes them feel stupid, and that's just not playing fair. Original Mad Man David Ogilvy said: "Never use jargon words like reconceptualize, demassification, attitudinally, judgmentally. They are hallmarks of a pretentious ass."

Sometimes you do things just because y o u c a n